T0109861

THE ILLUSTRATED
Walt Whitman

25 ESSENTIAL POEMS

EDITED BY

RYAN G.
VAN CLEAVE

MOON
SHOWER

Introduction and supplemental material © 2024 by Ryan G. Van Cleave

Published by Moonshower, an imprint of Bushel & Peck Books.
All rights reserved. No part of this publication may be reproduced
without written permission from the publisher.

Bushel & Peck Books is dedicated to fighting illiteracy all over the world.
For every book we sell, we donate one to a child in need——book for book.
To nominate a school or organization to receive free books,
please visit www.bushelandpeckbooks.com.

Design and illustration by David Miles.
Type set in Baskerville and Calder.
Collage illustrations were created digitally from various public domain works
and/or elements licensed from Shutterstock.com.

LCCN: 2023946746
ISBN: 978-1-63819-212-1

First Edition

Printed in China

1 3 5 7 9 10 8 6 4 2

Selections

COMMUNITY & SELF

LIFE & DEATH

SPIRIT & SKY

Welcome to the Illustrated Poets Collection! Here are three suggestions to help you make the most of this book.

SUGGESTION 1: Enjoy the poems. This seems far more important than trying to puzzle out what the author meant (or what other people believe the author meant).

SUGGESTION 2: Engage with the poems by asking questions. Here are three that should prove useful for any poem you encounter:

- *What do you notice about this poem?*
- *How does this poem make you feel?*
- *What else have you read/seen/experienced that connects with this poem?*

You'll also find individual questions suggested for each poem in this book.

SUGGESTION 3: Be your own boss. Read the poems in order or jump around as you see fit. Share them or savor them all by yourself. Say them aloud or whisper their words in your heart.

Poetry makes life better. There is NO wrong way to experience a poem.

So, read on, dear friend. And thank you for choosing poetry.

Ryan G. Van Cleave
Series Editor

PART I

Community & Self

I HEAR AMERICA SINGING

I hear America singing, the varied **carols** I hear,
Those of mechanics, each one singing his as it should be **blithe** and strong,
The carpenter singing his as he measures his plank or beam,
The **mason** singing his as he makes ready for work, or leaves off work,
The boatman singing what belongs to him in his boat, the deckhand singing on the
  steamboat deck,
The shoemaker singing as he sits on his bench, the hatter singing as he stands,
The wood-cutter's song, the ploughboy's on his way in the morning, or at noon
  intermission or at sundown,

The delicious singing of the mother, or of the young wife at work, or of the girl sewing or washing,
Each singing what belongs to him or her and to none else,
The day what belongs to the day—at night the party of young fellows, **robust**, friendly,
Singing with open mouths their strong melodious songs.

ENGAGE

What type of mood is created in the first few lines?

Why do you think Whitman chose to focus on ordinary people and their daily tasks?

Do you think these people are actually singing? If not, what might singing represent?

IMAGINE

If you were to add another verse to this poem, what other type of worker would you include and what would their song be like?

DEFINE

carols: *joyful songs*

blithe: *cheerful*

mason: *stoneworker*

robust: *strong and healthy*

SONG OF MYSELF
(5 EXCERPTS)

I.

I celebrate myself, and sing myself,
And what I assume you shall assume,
For every atom belonging to me as good belongs
   to you.

I **loafe** and invite my soul,
I lean and loafe at my ease observing a spear of
   summer grass.

My tongue, every atom of my blood, form'd
   from this soil, this air,
Born here of parents born here from parents the
   same, and their parents the same,
I, now thirty-seven years old in perfect health
   begin,
Hoping to cease not till death.

II.

My respiration and inspiration, the beating of
   my heart, the passing of blood and air through
   my lungs,
The sniff of green leaves and dry leaves, and of
   the shore and dark-color'd sea-rocks, and of
   hay in the barn,
The sound of the **belch'd** words of my voice
   loos'd to the **eddies** of the wind,
A few light kisses, a few embraces, a reaching
   around of arms,
The play of shine and shade on the trees as the
   supple **boughs** wag,
The delight alone or in the rush of the streets, or
   along the fields and hill-sides,
The feeling of health, the full-noon **trill**, the
   song of me rising from bed and meeting the
   sun.
Have you **reckon'd** a thousand acres much?

have you reckon'd the earth much?
Have you practis'd so long to learn to read?
Have you felt so proud to get at the meaning of
   poems?

Stop this day and night with me and you shall
   possess the origin of all poems,
You shall possess the good of the earth and sun,
   (there are millions of suns left,)
You shall no longer take things at second or third
   hand, nor look through the eyes of the dead, nor
   feed on the **spectres** in books,
You shall not look through my eyes either, nor take
   things from me,
You shall listen to all sides and filter them from
   your self.

VI.

A child said *What is the grass?* fetching it to me with
   full hands;
How could I answer the child? I do not know what
   it is any more than he.
I guess it must be the flag of my **disposition**,
   out of hopeful green stuff woven.

Or I guess it is the handkerchief of the Lord,
A scented gift and remembrancer designedly
   dropt,
Bearing the owner's name someway in the corners,
   that we may see and remark, and say *Whose?*

Or I guess the grass is itself a child, the produced
   babe of the vegetation.

LI.

The past and present **wilt**—I have fill'd them,
   emptied them.
And proceed to fill my next fold of the future.

Listener up there! what have you to **confide** to
   me?

Look in my face while I **snuff** the **sidle**
    of evening,
(Talk honestly, no one else hears you,
    and I stay only a minute longer.)
Do I **contradict** myself?
Very well then I contradict myself,
(I am large, I contain **multitudes**.)

LII.

The spotted hawk swoops by and
    accuses me, he complains of my
    gab and my loitering.

I too am not a bit tamed, I too am
    untranslatable,
I sound my **barbaric yawp** over the
    roofs of the world.

The last **scud** of day holds back for me,
It flings my likeness after the rest and true
    as any on the shadow'd wilds,
It coaxes me to the vapor and the dusk.

I depart as air, I shake my white locks at
    the runaway sun,
I **effuse** my flesh in eddies, and drift
    it in lacy **jags**.

I **bequeath** myself to the dirt to grow
    from the grass I love,
If you want me again look for me under
    your boot-soles.

You will hardly know who I am or what I
    mean,
But I shall be good health to you
    nevertheless,
And filter and fibre your blood.

Failing to fetch me at first keep encouraged,
Missing me one place search another,
I stop somewhere waiting for you.

ENGAGE

In the first excerpt, how does the speaker feel about himself and the world around him?

What does "I am large, I contain multitudes" mean to you?

The full version of "Song of Myself" is 52 sections and 1,300 lines. How fair is it to represent such a big poem with such small excerpts?

IMAGINE

Poems talk to each other in interesting ways. What does this one say to/about the next poem, which is "I Sing the Body Electric"?

DEFINE

loafe: *being lazy or relaxed*
belch'd: *loud burp*
eddies: *tiny whirlpools*
boughs: *main part of a tree*
trill: *quick vibrating sound*
reckon'd: *considered*
spectres: *ghosts*
disposition: *mood*
wilt: *wither*
confide: *share a secret*
snuff: *extinguish*
sidle: *approach unnoticed*
contradict: *express the opposite*
multitudes: *many or lots*
barbaric yawp: *loud, wild shout*
scud: *move fast in a straight line*
effuse: *spread out in all directions*
jags: *sharp, pointed edges*
bequeath: *give to someone after you die*

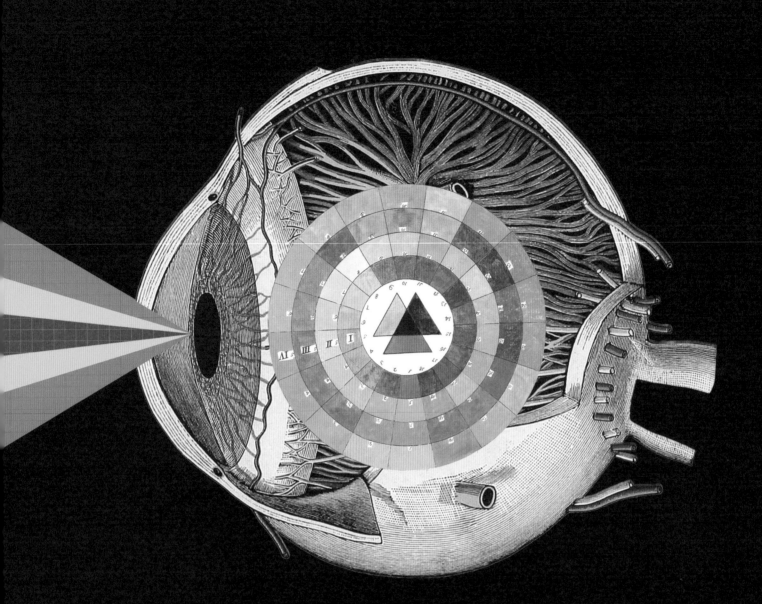

I SING THE
BODY ELECTRIC

(3 EXCERPTS)

I.

I sing the body electric,
The armies of those I love **engirth** me and
 I engirth them,
They will not let me off till I go with them,
 respond to them,

And **discorrupt** them, and charge them
 full with the charge of the soul.

Was it doubted that those who corrupt their
 own bodies conceal themselves?
And if those who **defile** the living are as
 bad as they who defile the dead?
And if the body does not do fully as much as
 the soul?
And if the body were not the soul, what is the
 soul?

II.

The expression of the face **balks** account,
But the expression of a well-made man appears not only
    in his face,
It is in his limbs and joints also, it is curiously in the
    joints of his hips and wrists,
It is in his walk, the carriage of his neck, the flex of his
    waist and knees, dress does not hide him,
The strong sweet quality he has strikes through the
    cotton and **broadcloth**,
To see him pass conveys as much as the best poem,
    perhaps more,
You linger to see his back, and the back of his neck and
    shoulder-side.

The sprawl and fulness of babes, the bosoms and heads
    of women, the folds of their dress, their style as we pass
    in the street, the contour of their shape downwards,
The swimmer naked in the swimming-bath, seen as he
    swims through the transparent green-shine, or lies with
    his face up and rolls silently to and fro in the heave of
    the water,
The bending forward and backward of rowers in row-
    boats, the horseman in his saddle,
Girls, mothers, house-keepers, in all their performances,
The group of laborers seated at noon-time with their
    open dinner-kettles, and their wives waiting,
The female soothing a child, the farmer's daughter in
    the garden or cow-yard,
The young fellow hoeing corn, the sleigh-driver driving
    his six horses through the crowd,
The wrestle of wrestlers, two apprentice-boys, quite
    grown, lusty, good-natured, native-born, out on the
    vacant lot at sun-down after work,
The coats and caps thrown down, the embrace of love
    and resistance,
The upper-hold and under-hold, the hair rumpled over
    and blinding the eyes;

ENGAGE

*How does Whitman
describe the human body
in these excerpts?*

*What parts of the
poem suggest that the
body and the soul are
interconnected?*

*Why do you think
Whitman might see
the human body as
"electric"?*

IMAGINE

*Make three statements
about this poem using
the words "could,"
"would," and "should."*

DEFINE

engirth: *surround*

discorrupt: *stop
decay*

defile: *ruin something*

balks: *stops*

broadcloth: *smooth
cloth*

The march of firemen in their own
costumes, the play of masculine
muscle through clean-setting
trowsers and waist-straps,
The slow return from the fire,
the pause when the bell strikes
suddenly again, and the listening
on the alert,
The natural, perfect, varied
attitudes, the bent head, the
curv'd neck and the counting;
Such-like I love—I loosen myself,
pass freely, am at the mother's
breast with the little child,
Swim with the swimmers, wrestle
with wrestlers, march in line with
the firemen, and pause, listen,
count.

VII.

A man's body at auction,
(For before the war I often go to the
slave-mart and watch the sale,)
I help the auctioneer, the **sloven**
does not half know his business.

Gentlemen look on this wonder,
Whatever the bids of the bidders
they cannot be high enough for it,
For it the globe lay preparing
quintillions of years without
one animal or plant,
For it the revolving cycles truly and
steadily roll'd.

In this head the all-baffling brain,
In it and below it the makings of
heroes.

Examine these limbs, red, black,
or white, they are **cunning** in
tendon and nerve,
They shall be stript that you may
see them.

Exquisite senses, life-lit eyes,
pluck, **volition**,
Flakes of breast-muscle, **pliant**
backbone and neck, flesh not
flabby, good-sized arms and legs,
And wonders within there yet.

Within there runs blood,
The same old blood! the same red-
running blood!
There swells and jets a heart, there
all passions, desires, reachings,
aspirations;
(Do you think they are not there
because they are not express'd in
parlors and lecture-rooms?)

This is not only one man, this
the father of those who shall be
fathers in their turns,
In him the start of populous states
and rich republics,
Of him countless immortal lives
with countless embodiments and
enjoyments.

How do you know who shall come
from the offspring of his offspring
through the centuries?
(Who might you find you have
come from yourself, if you could
trace back through the centuries?)

trowsers: *pants*

sloven: *messy person*

quintillions: *very large number*

cunning: *sneaky*

exquisite: *very beautiful*

pluck: *courage*

volition: *making a choice*

pliant: *easily changed*

ENGAGE

How does the speaker feel about life?

How does this poem explore the concept of someone's life's purpose?

Where do you find encouragement, resilience, and perseverance?

IMAGINE

How would the story of this poem be different if it were told from someone else's point of view?

DEFINE

reproaching: *disapproving*

vainly: *without success*

plodding: *move slowly*

sordid: *dirty, unpleasant*

verse: *poetry line*

O ME! O LIFE!

Oh me! Oh life! of the questions of these recurring,
Of the endless trains of the faithless, of cities fill'd with the foolish,
Of myself forever **reproaching** myself, (for who more foolish
    than I, and who more faithless?)
Of eyes that **vainly** crave the light, of the objects mean, of the
    struggle ever renew'd,
Of the poor results of all, of the **plodding** and **sordid** crowds I
    see around me,
Of the empty and useless years of the rest, with the rest me
    intertwined,
The question, O me! so sad, recurring—What good amid these, O
    me, O life?

Answer.
That you are here—that life exists and identity,
That the powerful play goes on, and you may contribute a **verse**.

13

CROSSING BROOKLYN FERRY

(3 EXCERPTS)

I.

Flood-tide below me! I see you face to face!
Clouds of the west—sun there half an hour
  high—I see you also face to face.

Crowds of men and women attired in the usual
  costumes, how curious you are to me!

On the ferry-boats the hundreds and hundreds
  that cross, returning home, are more curious to
  me than you suppose,
And you that shall cross from shore to shore
  years **hence** are more to me, and more in my
  meditations, than you might suppose.

II.

The **impalpable** sustenance of me from all
  things at all hours of the day,
The simple, compact, well-join'd scheme, myself
  disintegrated, every one disintegrated yet part of
  the scheme,
The **similitudes** of the past and those of the
  future,
The glories strung like beads on my smallest sights
  and hearings, on the walk in the street and the
  passage over the river,
The current rushing so swiftly and swimming with
  me far away,
The others that are to follow me, the ties between
  me and them,
The certainty of others, the life, love, sight, hearing
  of others.

Others will enter the gates of the ferry and
   cross from shore to shore,
Others will watch the run of the flood-tide,
Others will see the shipping of Manhattan north and west,
   and the heights of Brooklyn to the south and east,
Others will see the islands large and small;
Fifty years hence, others will see them as they cross,
   the sun half an hour high,
A hundred years hence, or ever so many hundred years hence,
   others will see them,
Will enjoy the sunset, the pouring-in of the flood-tide,
   the falling-back to the sea of the ebb-tide.

v.

What is it then between us?
What is the count of the **scores** or hundreds of years between us?

Whatever it is, it **avails** not—distance avails not,
   and place avails not,
I too lived, Brooklyn of ample hills was mine,
I too walk'd the streets of Manhattan island,
   and bathed in the waters around it,
I too felt the curious abrupt questionings stir within me,
In the day among crowds of people sometimes they came upon me,
In my walks home late at night or as I lay in
   my bed they came upon me,
I too had been struck from the float forever held in solution,
I too had receiv'd identity by my body,
That I was I knew was of my body, and what I
   should be I knew I should be of my body.

ENGAGE

What does the speaker observe from the ferry?

Why do you think Whitman chose a ferry crossing as a setting for this poem?

Anaphora is the repetition of initial words or phrases in a row, such as "Others will" and "I too." Why do you imagine Whitman used that technique here?

IMAGINE

If you could ask this poem's speaker three questions, what would you ask? What do you imagine the answers might be?

DEFINE

hence: *as a result*

impalpable: *can't be touched*

similitudes: *repetitions*

scores: *sets of twenty*

avails: *helps*

TO A STRANGER

Passing stranger! you do not know how longingly I look
  upon you,
You must be he I was seeking, or she I was seeking, (it
  comes to me as of a dream,)
I have somewhere surely lived a life of joy with you,
All is recall'd as we **flit** by each other, fluid,
  affectionate, **chaste**, matured,
You grew up with me, were a boy with me or a girl
  with me,
I ate with you and slept with you, your body has
  become not yours only nor left my body mine only,
You give me the pleasure of your eyes, face, flesh, as we
  pass, you take of my beard, breast, hands, in return,
I am not to speak to you, I am to think of you when I
  sit alone or wake at night alone,
I am to wait, I do not doubt I am to meet you again,
I am to see to it that I do not lose you.

ENGAGE

Why might the speaker feel so connected to the stranger?

What emotions do you think the speaker is feeling?

Why might Whitman choose to repeat "I am" in the final three lines?

IMAGINE

Write the story of this poem . . . in exactly seven words.

DEFINE

flit: *flutter*

chaste: *restrained, innocent*

SHUT NOT YOUR DOORS

Shut not your doors to me proud libraries,
For that which was lacking on all your well-fill'd shelves, yet
     needed most, I bring,
Forth from the war emerging, a book I have made,
The words of my book nothing, the drift of it every thing,
A book separate, not link'd with the rest nor felt by the intellect,
But you ye untold **latencies** will thrill to every page.

⚙ **ENGAGE**

What does the speaker want to be accepted by?

Why do you think the speaker is so determined not to be shut out?

How does Whitman express his desire to be part of something bigger?

💡 **IMAGINE**

Give this poem a theme song. What are your favorite options?

🔤 **DEFINE**

latencies: *present but not yet visible*

TO THE STATES

To the States or any one of them, or any city of the States, *Resist much, obey little,*
Once unquestioning obedience, once fully enslaved,
Once fully enslaved, no nation, state, city of this earth, ever afterward resumes its **liberty**.

What message might the speaker be trying to send to the states?

What might Whitman think is the role of individuals in shaping a country?

Which word or phrase resonates with you the most? Why?

IMAGINE

If you could send a message to your country or state, what would it be?

DEFINE

liberty: *freedom*

SONG OF THE OPEN ROAD

(3 EXCERPTS)

I.

Afoot and light-hearted I take to the open
  road,
Healthy, free, the world before me,
The long brown path before me leading
  wherever I choose.

Henceforth I ask not good-fortune, I
  myself am good-fortune,
Henceforth I whimper no more, postpone no
  more, need nothing,
Done with indoor complaints, libraries,
  querulous criticisms,
Strong and content I travel the open road.

The earth, that is sufficient,
I do not want the constellations any nearer,
I know they are very well where they are,
I know they **suffice** for those who belong
  to them.

(Still here I carry my old delicious burdens,
I carry them, men and women, I carry them
  with me wherever I go,
I swear it is impossible for me to get rid of
  them,
I am fill'd with them, and I will fill them in
  return.)

V.

From this hour I **ordain** myself loos'd of
  limits and imaginary lines,

Going where I list, my own master total and
  absolute,
Listening to others, considering well what
  they say,
Pausing, searching, receiving, contemplating,
Gently, but with undeniable will, divesting
  myself of the holds that would hold me.
I inhale great **draughts** of space,
The east and the west are mine, and the
  north and the south are mine.

I am larger, better than I thought,
I did not know I held so much goodness.

All seems beautiful to me,
I can repeat over to men and women You
  have done such good to me I would do the
  same to you,
I will recruit for myself and you as I go,
I will scatter myself among men and women
  as I go,
I will toss a new gladness and roughness
  among them,
Whoever denies me it shall not trouble me,
Whoever accepts me he or she shall be
  blessed and shall bless me.

XV.

Allons! the road is before us!
It is safe—I have tried it—my own feet have
  tried it well—be not **detain'd**!

Let the paper remain on the desk unwritten,
  and the book on the shelf unopen'd!
Let the tools remain in the workshop! let the
  money remain unearn'd!
Let the school stand! mind not the cry of the
  teacher!

Let the preacher preach in his **pulpit**! let the lawyer
  plead in the court, and the judge **expound** the law.

Camerado, I give you my hand!
I give you my love more precious than money,
I give you myself before preaching or law;
Will you give me yourself? will you come travel with me?
Shall we stick by each other as long as we live?

ENGAGE

*What do you think the open
road might represent?*

*How does the speaker feel
about their journey?*

*What words or phrases
in these excerpts suggest a
sense of freedom?*

IMAGINE

*Draw the map of this poem.
Include all the relevant
sites, stops, and secrets.*

DEFINE

henceforth: *from this
time on*

querulous: *always
whining*

suffice: *be enough*

ordain: *give orders*

draughts: *deep gulps*

allons: *French for "let's
go"*

detain'd: *held back*

pulpit: *raised church
platform*

expound: *explain in
detail*

camerado: *friend*

PART II

Life & Death

O CAPTAIN! MY CAPTAIN!

O Captain! my Captain! our fearful trip is done,
The ship has weather'd every **rack**, the prize we **sought** is won,
The port is near, the bells I hear, the people all **exulting**,
While follow eyes the steady **keel**, the vessel grim and daring;
But O heart! heart! heart!
O the bleeding drops of red,
Where on the deck my Captain lies,
Fallen cold and dead.

O Captain! my Captain! rise up and hear the bells;
Rise up—for you the flag is flung—for you the bugle **trills**,
For you bouquets and ribbon'd wreaths—for you the shores a-crowding,
For you they call, the swaying mass, their eager faces turning;
    Here Captain! dear father!
      This arm beneath your head!
       It is some dream that on the deck,
        You've fallen cold and dead.

My Captain does not answer, his lips are pale and still,
My father does not feel my arm, he has no pulse nor will,
The ship is anchor'd safe and sound, its voyage closed and done,
From fearful trip the victor ship comes in with object won;
    Exult O shores, and ring O bells!
      But I with mournful **tread**,
       Walk the deck my Captain lies,
        Fallen cold and dead.

ENGAGE

Why do you think the speaker refers to the leader as "Captain"?

How does the speaker describe the victory?

What words or phrases express the speaker's grief?

IMAGINE

What kind of soundtrack would go with this poem? What songs and sounds pair well with the story?

DEFINE

rack: *destructive winds*

sought: *looked for*

exulting: *showing joy*

keel: *long piece of wood or metal along the bottom of a boat*

trills: *quick vibrating sounds*

tread: *walk*

WHEN LILACS LAST IN THE DOORYARD BLOOM'D

(4 EXCERPTS)

I.

When lilacs last in the dooryard bloom'd,
And the great star early droop'd in the
   western sky in the night,
I mourn'd, and yet shall mourn with ever-
   returning spring.

Ever-returning spring, **trinity** sure to me
   you bring,
Lilac blooming **perennial** and drooping
   star in the west,
And thought of him I love.

II.

O powerful western fallen star!
O shades of night—O moody, tearful night!
O great star disappear'd—O the black murk
   that hides the star!
O cruel hands that hold me powerless—O
   helpless soul of me!
O harsh surrounding cloud that will not free
   my soul.

VI.

Coffin that passes through lanes and streets,
Through day and night with the great cloud
   darkening the land,
With the pomp of the **inloop'd** flags with
   the cities draped in black,
With the show of the States themselves as of
   crape-veil'd women standing,
With processions long and winding and the
   flambeaus of the night,
With the countless torches lit, with the silent
   sea of faces and the unbared heads,
With the waiting depot, the arriving coffin,
   and the **sombre** faces,
With **dirges** through the night, with the
   thousand voices rising strong and solemn,
With all the mournful voices of the dirges
   pour'd around the coffin,
The dim-lit churches and the shuddering
   organs—where amid these you journey,
With the tolling tolling bells' perpetual
   clang,
Here, coffin that slowly passes,
I give you my sprig of lilac.

X.

O how shall I warble myself for the dead one
   there I loved?
And how shall I deck my song for the large
   sweet soul that has gone?
And what shall my perfume be for the grave
   of him I love?

Sea-winds blown from east and west,
Blown from the Eastern sea and blown from
   the Western sea, till there on the prairies
   meeting,
These and with these and the breath of my
   chant,
I'll perfume the grave of him I love.

 ENGAGE

What do you think is the significance of the lilacs in these excerpts?

How does the speaker mourn the loss of the leader?

In the third excerpt, what words or phrases contribute to an overall sense of sorrow and mourning?

IMAGINE

Sometimes a poem is a window. Looking through the window of this poem, what do you see?

DEFINE

trinity: *group of three things*

perennial: *plants that live more than two years*

inloop'd: *coiled in loops*

crape-veil'd: *hidden by thin, crinkled fabric*

flambeaus: *flaming torches*

sombre: *dark, gloomy*

dirges: *funeral songs*

THE SHIP STARTING

Lo, the **unbounded** sea,
On its breast a ship starting, spreading all her sails, carrying even her **moonsails**,
The pennant is flying aloft, as she speeds she speeds so **stately**—below **emulous**
  waves press forward,
They surround the ship with shining curving motions and foam.

ENGAGE

What might the ship symbolize?

How is the ship's departure described?

Why might Whitman use so many S sounds here?

IMAGINE

If this poem were a question, what would it be asking? What's the answer?

DEFINE

unbounded: *without limits*

moonsails: *light square sails*

stately: *majestically*

emulous: *echoing*

BEAT! BEAT! DRUMS!

Beat! beat! drums!—blow! bugles! blow!
Through the windows—through doors—burst like a
    ruthless force,
Into the **solemn** church, and scatter the
    congregation,
Into the school where the scholar is studying;
Leave not the bridegroom quiet—no happiness must
    he have now with his bride,
Nor the peaceful farmer any peace, ploughing his
    field or gathering his grain,
So fierce you whirr and pound you drums—so
    shrill you bugles blow.

Beat! beat! drums!—blow! bugles! blow!
Over the traffic of cities—over the rumble of
    wheels in the streets;
Are beds prepared for sleepers at night in the
    houses? no sleepers must sleep in those beds,
No bargainers' bargains by day—no brokers
    or speculators—would they continue?
Would the talkers be talking? would the
    singer attempt to sing?
Would the lawyer rise in the court to state his
    case before the judge?
Then rattle quicker, heavier drums—you
    bugles wilder blow.

Beat! beat! drums!—blow! bugles! blow!
Make no **parley**—stop for no
    expostulation,
Mind not the timid—mind not the weeper or
    prayer,
Mind not the old man **beseeching** the
    young man,
Let not the child's voice be heard, nor the
    mother's **entreaties**,
Make even the **trestles** to shake the dead
    where they lie awaiting the **hearses**,
So strong you thump O terrible drums—so
    loud you bugles blow.

ENGAGE
_____

*How do the drums and
bugles disrupt daily life
in the poem?*

*What might the beating
drums symbolize?*

*Which words or
phrases express a sense
of urgency?*

IMAGINE
_____

*If you could add
another sound to the
noise of war in this
poem, what would it be
and why?*

DEFINE
_____

solemn: *serious*

shrill: *high, piercing
sound*

parley: *meeting
between enemies*

expostulation:
strong protest

beseeching:
begging

entreaties: *pleas*

trestles: *support
frames*

hearses: *vehicles that
carry a coffin*

ABOARD AT A SHIP'S HELM

Aboard, at a ship's **helm**,
A young steersman steering with care.

Through fog on a sea-coast **dolefully** ringing,
An ocean-bell—O a warning bell, rock'd by the waves.

O you give good notice indeed, you bell by the sea-reefs ringing,
Ringing, ringing, to warn the ship from its **wreck-place**.

For, as on the alert, O steersman, you mind the bell's **admonition**,
The bows turn, the **freighted** ship tacking speeds away under her gray sails,
The beautiful and noble ship with all her precious wealth speeds away **gayly** and safe.

But O the ship, the immortal ship! O ship aboard the ship!
Ship of the body, ship of the soul, voyaging, voyaging, voyaging.

ENGAGE

How is this journey at sea described?

What might the helm represent?

What are some of the challenges the ship faces at sea? What other challenges could it later face?

IMAGINE

If you were going to create a video to accompany the poem, what are some things you might include?

DEFINE

helm: *wheel that steers a ship*

dolefully: *very sadly*

wreck-place: *site of a catastrophe*

admonition: *warning*

freighted: *loaded with goods*

gayly: *happily*

PATROLING BARNEGAT

Wild, wild the storm, and the sea high running,
Steady the roar of the gale, with **incessant** undertone muttering,
Shouts of demoniac laughter fitfully piercing and **pealing**,
Waves, air, midnight, their savagest **trinity** lashing,
Out in the shadows there milk-white combs **careering**,
On beachy slush and sand spirts of snow fierce slanting,
Where through the murk the easterly death-wind **breasting**,
Through cutting swirl and spray watchful and firm advancing,
(That in the distance! is that a wreck? is the red signal flaring?)
Slush and sand of the beach tireless till daylight **wending**,
Steadily, slowly, through hoarse roar never **remitting**,
Along the midnight edge by those milk-white combs careering,
A group of dim, weird forms, struggling, the night confronting,
That savage trinity warily watching.

ENGAGE

What role might the lighthouse play in this poem?

How does the speaker portray the power of nature?

Why might all the last words in each line end with -ing?

IMAGINE

What's another title you could give this poem?

DEFINE

Barnegat: *bay on the east coast of New Jersey*

incessant: *continuous*

pealing: *loud bell ringing*

trinity: *group of three*

careering: *uncontrolled movement*

breasting: *moving through something*

wending: *walking*

remitting: *easing off*

COME UP FROM THE FIELDS FATHER

Come up from the fields father, here's a letter
    from our Pete,
And come to the front door mother, here's a
    letter from thy dear son.

Lo, 'tis autumn,
Lo, where the trees, deeper green, yellower
    and redder,
Cool and sweeten Ohio's villages with leaves
    fluttering in the moderate wind,

Where apples ripe in the orchards hang and
    grapes on the **trellis'd** vines,
(Smell you the smell of the grapes on the
    vines?
Smell you the buckwheat where the bees
    were lately buzzing?)

Above all, lo, the sky so calm, so transparent
    after the rain, and with wondrous clouds,
Below too, all calm, all vital and beautiful,
    and the farm prospers well.

Down in the fields all prospers well,
But now from the fields come father, come at
    the daughter's call,
And come to the entry mother, to the front
    door come right away.

Fast as she can she hurries, something
    ominous, her steps trembling,
She does not **tarry** to smooth her hair nor
    adjust her cap.

38

Open the envelope quickly,
O this is not our son's writing, yet his name is sign'd,
O a strange hand writes for our dear son, O **stricken**
  mother's soul!
All swims before her eyes, flashes with black, she catches
  the main words only,
Sentences broken, *gunshot wound in the breast, cavalry*
  skirmish, *taken to hospital,*
At present low, but will soon be better.

Ah now the single figure to me,
Amid all **teeming** and wealthy Ohio with all its cities
  and farms,
Sickly white in the face and dull in the head, very faint,
By the **jamb** of a door leans.

Grieve not so, dear mother, (the just-grown daughter speaks
  through her sobs,
The little sisters huddle around speechless and dismay'd,)
See, dearest mother, the letter says Pete will soon be better.
Alas poor boy, he will never be better, (nor may-be needs
  to be better, that brave and simple soul,)
While they stand at home at the door he is dead already,
The only son is dead.

But the mother needs to be better,
She with thin form presently **drest** in black,
By day her meals untouch'd, then at night fitfully
  sleeping, often waking,
In the midnight waking, weeping, longing with one deep
  longing,
O that she might withdraw unnoticed, silent from life
  escape and withdraw,
To follow, to seek, to be with her dear dead son.

How does the speaker describe the impact of war on a family?

How does the tone of the poem change after the letter arrives?

What emotions do you think the family is feeling?

 IMAGINE

If you had to assign each stanza a color, what would you choose? Why?

DEFINE

lo: *expression of surprise*

trellis'd: *supported with light bars*

ominous: *menacing*

tarry: *delay*

stricken: *deeply hurt*

skirmish: *quick battle*

teeming: *full of activity*

jamb: *side of an opening*

drest: *dressed*

PART III

Spirit & Sky

A NOISELESS PATIENT SPIDER

A noiseless patient spider,
I mark'd where on a little **promontory**
  it stood isolated,
Mark'd how to explore the **vacant** vast
  surrounding,
It launch'd forth **filament**, filament,
  filament, out of itself,
Ever unreeling them, ever tirelessly
  speeding them.

And you O my soul where you stand,
Surrounded, detached, in measureless
  oceans of space,
Ceaselessly **musing**, venturing,
  throwing, seeking the **spheres** to
  connect them,
Till the bridge you will need be form'd, till
  the **ductile** anchor hold,
Till the **gossamer** thread you fling
  catch somewhere, O my soul.

ENGAGE

Why might the spider be described as "noiseless" and "patient"?

What might the spider's web symbolize?

How does this poem make you feel? What about the poem contributes to that feeling?

IMAGINE

If you could talk to the spider, what would you say or ask? What do you think the spider might say back?

DEFINE

promontory: *high point of land*

vacant: *empty*

filament: *threadlike object*

musing: *thinking deeply*

spheres: *planets*

ductile: *able to bend without breaking*

gossamer: *light, thin, delicate*

WHEN I HEARD THE LEARN'D ASTRONOMER

When I heard the **learn'd** astronomer,
When the proofs, the figures, were **ranged** in
   columns before me,
When I was shown the charts and diagrams, to add,
   divide, and measure them,
When I sitting heard the astronomer where he
   lectured with much applause in the lecture-room,
How soon unaccountable I became tired and sick,
Till rising and gliding out I wander'd off by myself,
In the mystical moist night-air, and from time to time,
Look'd up in perfect silence at the stars.

ENGAGE

What contrasts do you find between the astronomer's lecture and the speaker's own experience of the stars?

What might the stars represent for the speaker?

How does Whitman use repetition in this poem, and what effect does it create?

IMAGINE

Read this poem every day for a week. What new details or nuances do you notice as you re-encounter the poem each time?

DEFINE

learn'd: *educated*

ranged: *arranged*

THOUGHTS

(4 EXCERPTS)

I.

OF the **visages** of things—And of piercing through
to the accepted hells beneath;

Of ugliness—To me there is just as much in it as there
is in beauty—And now the ugliness of human beings
is acceptable to me;

Of detected persons—To me, detected persons are not,
in any respect, worse than undetected persons—and
are not in any respect worse than I am myself;

Of criminals—To me, any judge, or any juror, is
equally criminal—and any reputable person is also—
and the President is also.

II.

OF waters, forests, hills;

Of the earth at large, whispering through medium of
me;

Of vista—Suppose some sight in **arriere**, through
the formative chaos, presuming the growth, fulness,
life, now attain'd on the journey;

(But I see the road continued, and the journey ever
continued;)

Of what was once lacking on earth, and in due time
has become supplied—And of what will yet be
supplied,

Because all I see and know, I believe to have **purport**
in what will yet be supplied.

V.

As I sit with others, at a great feast, suddenly, while the
    music is playing,
To my mind, (whence it comes I know not,) spectral, in
    mist, of a wreck at sea,
Of the flower of the marine science of fifty generations,
    founder'd off the Northeast coast, and going
    down—Of the steamship Arctic going down,
Of the **veil'd tableau**—Women gather'd together on
    deck, pale, heroic, waiting the moment that draws so
    close—O the moment!
O the huge sob—A few bubbles—the white foam
    spirting up—And then the women gone,
Sinking there, while the passionless wet flows on—And
    I now pondering, Are those women indeed gone?
Are Souls drown'd and destroy'd so?
Is only matter triumphant?

VI.

OF what I write from myself—As if that were not the
    resumé;
Of Histories—As if such, however complete, were not
    less complete than my poems;
As if the shreds, the records of nations, could possibly
    be as lasting as my poems;
As if here were not the amount of all nations, and of all
    the lives of heroes.

ENGAGE

*How does Whitman
describe his thoughts in
this poem?*

*Whitman mentions a
shipwreck in this poem.
Why do you think
he included this sad
moment?*

*What might the
speaker be searching for
in this poem?*

IMAGINE

*If your thoughts could
take physical form,
what would they look
like and why?*

DEFINE

visages: *faces or
appearances*

arriere: *view of the
past*

purport: *main idea*

founder'd: *fill with
water and sink*

veil'd tableau:
partially covered picture

resumé: *summary of
accomplishments*

OUT OF THE CRADLE ENDLESSLY ROCKING

(3 EXCERPTS)

(EXCERPT ONE)

Once **Paumanok**,

When the lilac-scent was in the air and Fifth-
  month grass was growing,

Up this seashore in some **briers**,

Two feather'd guests from Alabama, two
  together,

And their nest, and four light-green eggs spotted
  with brown,

And every day the he-bird to and fro near at
  hand,

And every day the she-bird crouch'd on her nest,
  silent, with bright eyes,

And every day I, a curious boy, never too close,
  never disturbing them,

Cautiously peering, absorbing, translating.

Shine! shine! shine!
Pour down your warmth, great sun!
*While we **bask**, we two together.*

Two together!
Winds blow south, or winds blow north,
Day come white, or night come black,
Home, or rivers and mountains from home,
Singing all time, minding no time,
While we two keep together.

(EXCERPT TWO)

The **aria** sinking,

All else continuing, the stars shining,

The winds blowing, the notes of the bird
  continuous echoing,

With angry moans the fierce old mother
  incessantly moaning,

On the sands of Paumanok's shore gray and
  rustling,

The yellow half-moon enlarged, sagging down,
  drooping, the face of the sea almost touching,

The boy ecstatic, with his bare feet the waves,
  with his hair the atmosphere **dallying**,

The love in the heart long pent, now loose, now
  at last **tumultuously** bursting,

The aria's meaning, the ears, the soul, swiftly
  depositing,

The strange tears down the cheeks coursing,

The **colloquy** there, the trio, each uttering,

The undertone, the savage old mother
  incessantly crying,

To the boy's soul's questions **sullenly** timing,
  some drown'd secret hissing,

To the **outsetting bard**.

(EXCERPT THREE)

O you singer solitary, singing by yourself,
  projecting me,

O solitary me listening, never more shall I cease
  perpetuating you,

Never more shall I escape, never more the
  reverberations,

Never more the cries of unsatisfied love be
  absent from me,

Never again leave me to be the peaceful child I
  was before what there in the night,

By the sea under the yellow and sagging moon,

The messenger there arous'd, the fire, the sweet
  hell within,

The unknown want, the destiny of me.

O give me the **clew**! (it lurks in the night here
  somewhere,)

O if I am to have so much, let me have more!

What significance might the "two feather'd guests from Alabama" (birds) hold in the poem?

How does the imagery of the sea throughout these excerpts contribute to its overall themes and mood?

Whitman's poetry often sounds like music. Where do you see language that is rhythmic or melodic? What do you think he chose to write this way?

IMAGINE

If this poem were an egg, what might hatch from it if it got enough warmth and attention?

DEFINE

Paumanok: *Long Island, New York*

briers: *thorny plants*

bask: *enjoy warmth*

aria: *song in an opera*

dallying: *playing around*

tumultuously: *wild, noisy way*

colloquy: *conversation*

sullenly: *acting grumpy*

outsetting: *beginning*

bard: *poet*

perpetuating: *making something last forever*

reverberations: *echoes*

clew: *clue*

49

I SAW IN LOUISIANA A LIVE-OAK GROWING

I saw in Louisiana a **live-oak** growing,
All alone stood it and the moss hung down from the
   branches,
Without any companion it grew there **uttering** joyous
   leaves of dark green,
And its look, rude, unbending, **lusty**, made me think of
   myself,
But I wonder'd how it could utter joyous leaves standing
   alone there without its friend near, for I knew I could not,
And I broke off a twig with a certain number of leaves upon
   it, and twined around it a little moss,
And brought it away, and I have placed it in sight in my
   room,
It is not needed to remind me as of my own dear friends,
(For I believe lately I think of little else than of them,)
Yet it remains to me a curious token, it makes me think of
   manly love;
For all that, and though the live-oak glistens there in
   Louisiana solitary in a wide flat space,
Uttering joyous leaves all its life without a friend a lover near,
I know very well I could not.

⚙ ENGAGE

Why do you think the speaker feels a connection with the live-oak tree?

How do Whitman's reflections on the live-oak tree contribute to themes about nature and human life?

There's punctuation at the end of every line. How does that affect the poem's reading? Its meaning?

💡 IMAGINE

Find a tree or plant in your neighborhood or a nearby park. Observe it closely. How does it make you feel? Does it remind you of anything?

🅰 DEFINE

live-oak: *type of tree that stays green throughout the year*

uttering: *saying*

lusty: *full of energy*

A CLEAR MIDNIGHT

This is thy hour O Soul, thy free flight into the wordless,
Away from books, away from art, the day erased, the lesson done,
Thee fully forth emerging, silent, gazing, **pondering** the themes thou lovest best,
Night, sleep, death and the stars.

ENGAGE

What do you think the speaker is thinking about during this hour?

What might "free flight into the wordless" mean?

What does the speaker truly feel about night, sleep, death, and the stars?

IMAGINE

Respond to this poem in art. Use paint, chalk, pencils, or crayons to express the emotions and illustrate the imagery.

DEFINE

pondering:
thinking about

On the beach at night,
Stands a child with her father,
Watching the east, the autumn sky.

Up through the darkness,
While **ravening** clouds, the burial clouds, in black masses spreading,
Lower **sullen** and fast **athwart** and down the sky,
Amid a transparent clear belt of **ether** yet left in the east,
Ascends large and calm the lord-star **Jupiter**,
And **nigh at hand**, only a very little above,
Swim the delicate sisters the **Pleiades**.

From the beach the child holding the hand of her father,
Those burial-clouds that lower victorious soon to devour all,
Watching, silently weeps.

Weep not, child,
Weep not, my darling,
With these kisses let me remove your tears,
The ravening clouds shall not long be victorious,
They shall not long possess the sky, they devour the stars only in **apparition**,
Jupiter shall emerge, be patient, watch again another night, the Pleiades shall emerge,
They are immortal, all those stars both silvery and golden shall shine out again,
The great stars and the little ones shall shine out again, they endure,
The vast immortal suns and the long-enduring **pensive** moons shall again shine.

Then dearest child mournest thou only for Jupiter?
Considerest thou alone the burial of the stars?

Something there is,
(With my lips soothing thee, adding I whisper,
I give thee the first suggestion, the problem and indirection,)
Something there is more immortal even than the stars,
(Many the burials, many the days and nights, passing away,)
Something that shall endure longer even than **lustrous** Jupiter
Longer than sun or any revolving satellite,
Or the radiant sisters the Pleiades.

ENGAGE

How does the speaker comfort the little girl in the poem?

What do you make of parenthetical lines (language within parentheses—like this!) in a poem?

What role does nature seem to play in this poem?

IMAGINE

If you could gaze at the stars with the speaker, what questions would you ask?

DEFINE

ravening: *very hungry*

sullen: *gloomily*

athwart: *across*

ether: *clear sky; the upper regions of air beyond the clouds*

Jupiter: *largest planet in our solar system*

nigh at hand: *near*

Pleiades: *group of stars in the constellation Taurus*

apparition: *ghost or ghostlike image*

pensive: *thoughtful*

lustrous: *shining*

I DREAMED IN A DREAM

I dream'd in a dream, I saw a city **invincible** to the attacks of the whole of the rest of the earth;

I dream'd that was the new city of Friends,

Nothing was greater there than the quality of **robust** love, it led the rest;

It was seen every hour in the actions of the men of that city,

And in all their looks and words.

ENGAGE

What effect does the repetition of dreams have on the poem?

How does the varying line length affect your reading of the poem?

Why do think Whitman chose such clear, direct language?

IMAGINE

If you could rename the city of Friends based on your own dream city, what would you call it? Why?

DEFINE

invincible:
unbeatable

robust: *strong and healthy*

Poets to come! **orators**, singers, musicians to come!
Not to-day is to justify me and answer what I am for,
But you, a new **brood**, native, athletic, **continental**, greater than before known,
Arouse! for you must justify me.

I myself but write one or two **indicative** words for the future,
I but advance a moment only to wheel and hurry back in the darkness.

I am a man who, **sauntering** along without fully stopping, turns a casual look
   upon you and then **averts** his face,
Leaving it to you to prove and define it,
Expecting the main things from you.

ENGAGE

What is the speaker's message to future poets?

How does Whitman perceive his own role as a poet?

What hopes and expectations does the speaker have for the poets of the future?

 IMAGINE

Imagine you're a future poet that Whitman is addressing. What would you want to tell him about the future of poetry?

 DEFINE

orators: *speakers*

brood: *generation*

continental: *relating to a continent*

indicative: *serving to point out*

sauntering: *walking leisurely*

averts: *turn away*

Ten Things to Know about Walt Whitman

1. The second oldest of nine children, Walt Whitman (1819–1892) was one of the most famous American poets of the 19th century.

2. To help provide for his large family, he quit school at eleven years old and got a job as an office boy for two lawyers before working as a teacher, printer, and journalist.

3. He had a long, graying beard and was six feet tall, which was especially tall for that time.

4. When his brother was wounded in the American Civil War, Whitman visited him and was so affected that he volunteered to care for wounded soldiers.

5. In 1855, he self-published the first edition of his poetry book, *Leaves of Grass*. It only had twelve poems—though some were quite long.

6. He worked on *Leaves of Grass* over his entire lifetime. Upon his death, the book contained around 400 poems.

7. He never married. Most scholars believe he was homosexual, though he kept that a secret from nearly everyone.

8. The author of *Dracula*, Bram Stoker, was a huge fan of Whitman. He and his friends even called themselves "Walt Whitmanites."

9. While some critics and writers of the time applauded his poetry, many found it scandalous both for its frankness about religion, death, and sexuality as well as for how he departed from well-established traditions of poetry.

10. He's often considered to be the father of free verse poetry, meaning poems that don't use traditional rhyme or meter (sound patterns).

Commentary on the Poems

PART I: COMMUNITY & SELF

"I Hear America Singing"
This poem celebrates the individual voices of American workers, each singing their unique song, yet harmoniously building the American symphony.

NOTICE HOW THE POEM DOESN'T MERELY DESCRIBE THE WORK, BUT GIVES EACH TASK A SONG, EMPHASIZING THE DIGNITY AND IMPORTANCE OF ALL LABOR.

"Song of Myself" (5 excerpts)
The speaker, Whitman himself, celebrates the wonders of nature and the connection between the self and the natural world.

NOTICE HOW THIS IS A FREE VERSE POEM, WHICH MEANS IT DOESN'T HAVE A SET RHYME OR RHYTHM. DOES THAT SYMBOLIZE INDIVIDUAL FREEDOM AND EXPRESSION?

"I Sing the Body Electric" (3 excerpts)
Whitman sees the human body as a sacred object, celebrating its physical and sensual attributes.

NOTICE HOW THE LONG LISTS CAPTURE THE VARIETY AND COMPLEXITY OF THE HUMAN BODY, SHOWING HIS DEEP APPRECIATION FOR ITS BEAUTY.

"O Me! O Life!"
Whitman asks existential questions about life's purpose but answers them with the promise of each individual's potential.

NOTICE HOW HE TURNS THE INDIVIDUAL'S CRISIS INTO A COLLECTIVE ONE, SUGGESTING THAT WE ALL SHARE THE SAME QUESTIONS.

"Crossing Brooklyn Ferry"
(3 excerpts)
This poem establishes a spiritual connection between the past, present, and future, as the speaker contemplates the unchanging natural elements.

NOTICE HOW WHITMAN CREATES A FEELING OF TIMELESSNESS BY IMAGINING FUTURE READERS EXPERIENCING THE SAME FERRY RIDE.

"To a Stranger"
The speaker feels a deep connection with a stranger, suggesting a shared humanity.

NOTICE HOW WHITMAN CONNECTS WITH THE READER THROUGH THE REPETITION OF "YOU" AND "I."

"Shut Not Your Doors"
The speaker pleads for acceptance and understanding, highlighting his vision of an open and inclusive America.

NOTICE HOW WHITMAN USES DOORS AS A METAPHOR FOR THE MINDS AND HEARTS OF HIS READERS, ADVISING THEM TO KEEP AN OPEN MIND.

"To the States"
Whitman addresses the American states, urging them to uphold democratic values and resist corruption.

NOTICE HOW WHITMAN PERSONIFIES THE STATES, DEMONSTRATING HIS BELIEF IN THE IMPORTANCE OF EACH STATE'S ROLE IN DEMOCRACY.

"Song of the Open Road" (3 excerpts)
This poem celebrates the freedom and possibilities of life's journey, metaphorically depicted as an open road.

NOTICE HOW WHITMAN EMPLOYS ANAPHORA, REPEATING THE PHRASE "ALL SEEMS BEAUTIFUL TO ME," TO EMPHASIZE HIS OPTIMISM AND POSITIVE OUTLOOK.

PART TWO: LIFE & DEATH

"O Captain! My Captain!"
Whitman mourns the death of President Abraham Lincoln, using the metaphor of a ship's captain to represent the late president.

NOTICE THE DRAMATIC SHIFT IN TONE FROM JUBILANT TO SORROWFUL, MIRRORING THE NATION'S MOOD AT THE END OF THE CIVIL WAR AND AFTER LINCOLN'S ASSASSINATION.

"When Lilacs Last in the Dooryard Bloom'd" (4 excerpts)
Like the previous poem, this is a lament about the profound loss of President Abraham Lincoln.

NOTICE HOW LILACS — WHICH WERE IN BLOOM DURING LINCOLN'S FUNERAL — BECOME A SYMBOL OF THE NATION'S SUFFERING.

"The Ship Starting"
Filled with emotions of anticipation and excitement, the speaker watches a ship embark on its journey.

NOTICE HOW WHITMAN CREATES A VIVID PICTURE OF THE SHIP'S DEPARTURE THROUGH SENSORY LANGUAGE, IMMERSING THE READER IN THE SCENE.

"Beat! Beat! Drums!"
Whitman depicts the disruptive power of war through the relentless beating of drums.

NOTICE HOW HE USES ONOMATOPOEIA, WORDS THAT SOUND LIKE WHAT THEY MEAN, TO CREATE A SENSE OF URGENCY AND CHAOS.

"Aboard at a Ship's Helm"
The poem captures the thrill of being at the helm of a ship, symbolizing life's journey.

NOTICE HOW WHITMAN USES MARITIME (CONNECTED WITH THE SEA) LANGUAGE TO ILLUSTRATE A SENSE OF CONTROL AND ADVENTURE.

"Patroling Barnegat"
Whitman describes a fierce storm off the coast of New Jersey, emphasizing the powerful, uncontrollable nature of the sea.

NOTICE HOW REPETITION AND POWERFUL ADJECTIVES SHOW THE CHAOTIC AND DANGEROUS ATMOSPHERE OF THE STORM.

"Come Up from the Fields Father"
This poem tells the tragic story of a family receiving news of their son's death in war.

NOTICE HOW WHITMAN USES SIMPLE, DIRECT LANGUAGE TO CONVEY THE DEEP SORROW OF LOSS.

"A Noiseless Patient Spider"

Whitman uses the metaphor of a spider spinning a web to explore themes of connection and exploration.

NOTICE HOW HE USES THE IMAGERY OF THE SOLITARY SPIDER TO SYMBOLIZE THE HUMAN SOUL'S SEARCH FOR MEANINGFUL CONNECTIONS.

"When I Heard the Learn'd Astronomer"

The speaker grows tired of an astronomer's factual lecture, finding more joy and understanding in experiencing the night sky directly.

NOTICE HOW WHITMAN CONTRASTS THE SCIENTIFIC LECTURE WITH THE SPEAKER'S PERSONAL EXPERIENCE TO EMPHASIZE THE IMPORTANCE OF INDIVIDUAL DISCOVERY.

"Thoughts" (4 excerpts)

This poem presents Whitman's meditative thoughts on nature, human life, and the universe.

NOTICE THE REFLECTIVE TONE WHITMAN USES, WHICH MIGHT INVITE READERS TO PONDER THEIR OWN THOUGHTS AND EXPERIENCES.

"Out of the Cradle Endlessly Rocking" (3 excerpts)

The speaker recalls a childhood memory of witnessing two lovebirds, which awakens his own understanding of love and loss.

NOTICE HOW A CRADLE SYMBOLIZES THE BIRTH OF THE SPEAKER'S POETIC VOICE.

"I Saw in Louisiana a Live-Oak Growing"

The speaker envies the independence of a solitary oak tree, yearning for a similar sense of contentment.

NOTICE HOW WHITMAN USES THE OAK TREE AS A SYMBOL OF SELF-RELIANCE AND FULFILLMENT IN SOLITUDE.

"A Clear Midnight"

This poem calls for a quiet moment for deep thoughts about big ideas like night, sleep, death, and stars.

NOTICE WHITMAN'S "LIST" IN THE LAST LINE. THIS TECHNIQUE HELPS POETS EMPHASIZE IMPORTANT IDEAS.

"On the Beach at Night"

This poem depicts a scene of a father comforting his daughter during a night at the beach, using it to explore themes of fear, comfort, and the infinite universe.

NOTICE HOW WHITMAN UTILIZES THE VASTNESS OF THE NIGHT SKY TO EMPHASIZE THE SMALLNESS YET SIGNIFICANCE OF HUMAN EXISTENCE.

"I Dreamed in a Dream"

Whitman shares his dream of an idyllic city that is built on the foundation of love and friendship, resisting all forms of aggression.

NOTICE HOW THE POEM IS A SINGLE, UNINTERRUPTED STANZA, REFLECTING THE CONTINUOUS FLOW OF A DREAM.

"Poets to Come"

Whitman addresses future poets, passing the poetic torch to them, and expressing his hopes for their work.

NOTICE HOW HE CREATES A SENSE OF UNITY AND CONTINUITY ACROSS GENERATIONS, EMPHASIZING THE ONGOING, COLLECTIVE HUMAN EXPERIENCE.

To Learn More about Walt Whitman

1   *Walt Whitman: Words for America* by Barbara Kerley, illustrated by Brian Selznick. Scholastic Press, 2004.

2   *Who Was Walt Whitman?* by Kirsten Anderson, illustrated by Tim Foley. Penguin Workshop, 2021.

Bibliography

1   www.poetryfoundation.org/poets/walt-whitman

2   www.poets.org/poet/walt-whitman

3   www.whitmanarchive.org

4   *Walt Whitman: Poetry and Prose*. Edited by Justin Kaplan. Library of America, 1996.

Special thanks to Dr. Matt Miller (Yeshiva University) for reviewing this manuscript.

ABOUT THE AUTHOR

Ryan G. Van Cleave wrote his first poem at age five, and he's been writing, reading, and loving poetry ever since. He earned a Ph.D. in American Literature with an emphasis in poetry and has taught literature and writing at numerous colleges and universities. Currently, he runs the creative writing major at Ringling College of Art and Design. As The Picture Book Whisperer, he helps celebrities write stories for kids and bring them to life on the page, stage, and screen.

www.ryangvancleave.com
www.thepicturebookwhisperer.com

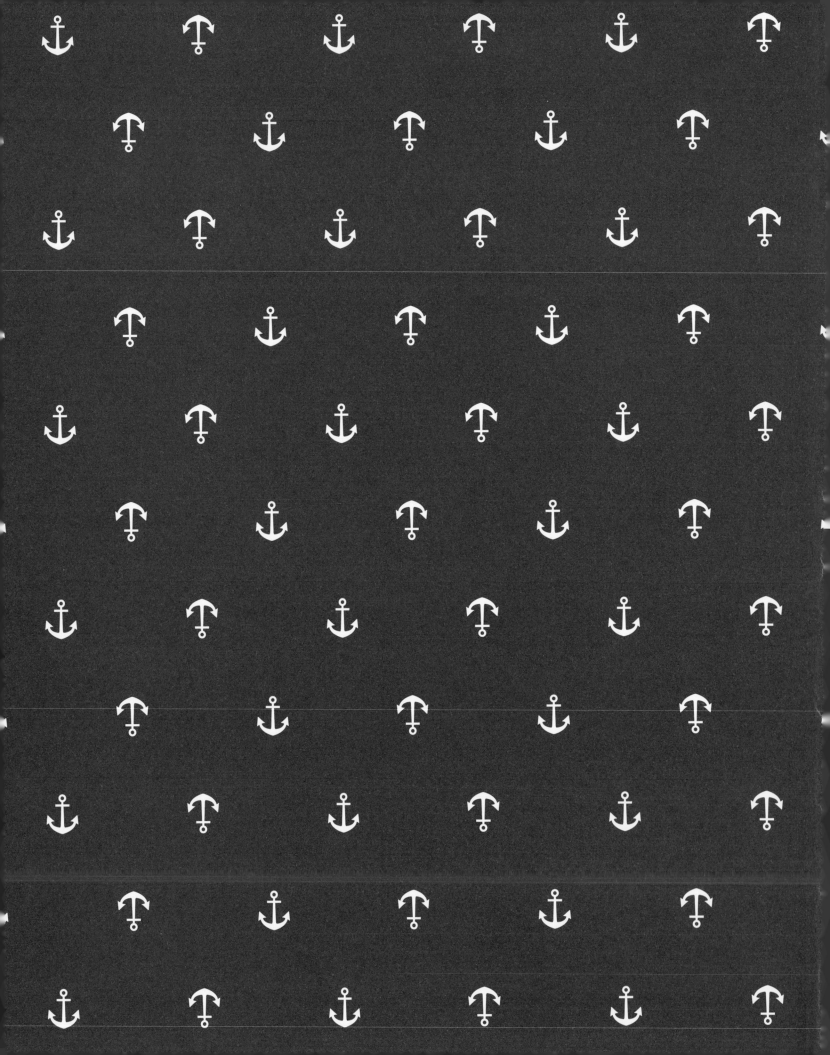